SALICYLATE

SENSITIVITY

COOKBOOK

Practical Guidance and Delicious Recipes for Embracing a Salicylate sensitivity or intolerance Lifestyle.

Curnow k. Rivers

DISCLAIMER NOTICE:

Please keep in mind that the information in this booklet is solely for educational and entertainment purposes. Every effort has been made to offer complete, accurate, and up to date information.

There are no express or implied guarantees of any kind. Readers understand that the author is not providing legal, financial, medical, or other professional advice.

TABLE OF CONTENTS

INTRODUCTION

Monica discovered that she was trapped in an unanticipated twist in the fabric of her life, a dance with a new partner that was referred to as salicylate sensitivity. The realization took her by surprise and sent her into a spiral of uncertainty and health problems. It was evident that Monica was struggling. Managing her health turned into a daily jigsaw puzzle as she struggled to distinguish between meals that nourished her body and those that made her more sensitive. She was desperate for a way to take back control because every meal seemed like a gamble.

In the middle of the conflict, the Healthy Meals Cookbook became an incredible resource. It was Monica's go to tool for battling salicylate sensitivity; it was much more than simply a cookbook. Not only did the cookbook provide meals, but it also turned into her ally and road map back to a flavorful existence.

In those pages, Monica found not only mouthwatering recipes but also a guide to achieving individual liberty. With her newly acquired confidence, she made the everyday spectacular by navigating the world of cuisine. The booklet served as Monica's pass to a victorious return and was much more than simply a cookbook.

Monica's journey is a tale of tenacity, self-discovery, and the triumph of flavor against salicylate sensitivity. Her tale echoes through these pages, calling to everyone who yearns for a tasty, salicylate friendly revolution as well as a satisfying lunch.

CHAPTER 1

UNDERSTANDING SALICYLATE SENSITIVITY

Welcome to the voyage into the delicate domain of salicylate sensitivity, an often-overlooked component of health that needs our attention. This chapter functions as a compass, leading readers through the complexity of salicylate sensitivity and building a firm basis for effective management.

INTRODUCTION TO SALICYLIC ACID

Salicylic acid, a naturally occurring chemical, has broad roots in both the synthetic and natural world. As a major component in numerous pharmaceuticals, cosmetic products, and a myriad of fruits and vegetables, its presence is far reaching. Salicylic acid's activity as a plant hormone and its effect in human physiology, notably in inflammatory processes, comprise the core of its relevance. This section uncovers the multidimensional character of salicylic acid, providing as a forerunner to understanding its influence on sensitive individuals.

CAUSES OF SALICYLATE SENSITIVITY

Salicylate sensitivity is typically a result of a complex combination of hereditary and environmental variables. Genetic predispositions regulating the activity of enzymes involved for salicylate metabolism play a critical role. Environmental variables, such exposure to particular-drugs or high salicylate diets, can function as triggers. In this section, we go into the subtle reasons, studying the genetic and environmental variables that lead to the development of sensitivity.

1. **MOLECULAR DETERMINANTS:** Genetic Predispositions

At the cellular level, genetic predispositions play a major role in defining an individual's vulnerability to salicylate sensitivity. Specific genetic variants can impact the activity of enzymes involved in salicylate metabolism. Enzymes such as UDP glucuronosyltransferases (UGTs) and glycine conjugation enzymes are vital in breaking down salicylates within the body. Genetic variations in the efficiency of these enzymes can contribute to an individual's predisposition to acquire sensitivity.

Exploring these genetic subtleties throws insight on the customized component of salicylate sensitivity, underlining that its presentation is not a one size fits all scenario.

2. **ENVIRONMENTAL DETERMINANTS: Triggers and Exposures**

Environmental variables also play an important role in the development of salicylate sensitivity. A diet heavy in foods containing salicylates or prolonged exposure to high dosages of salicylates from some drugs might serve as triggers. Aspirin and other non-steroidal anti-inflammatory medicines (NSAIDs) are examples of medications that include salicylates, which might increase a person's threshold for sensitivity. A diet rich in fruits, vegetables, spices, and even certain plants might expose people to elevated salicylate levels. Recognizing and understanding these environmental variables is critical for preventing and controlling the emergence of sensitivity.

3. **IMMUNOLOGICAL CONSIDERATIONS: A Closer Look at Immune Responses**

Immunological considerations also play a role in the development of salicylate sensitivity, in addition to molecular and environmental variables.

Individuals' immunological responses to salicylates might differ. In rare situations, an overactive immune response may cause sensitivity related symptoms.

This complexity of immunological processes adds another level to the complex process of developing sensitivity.

4. INTERPLAY OF FACTORS: A Holistic View

Crucially, an individual's vulnerability to salicylate sensitivity is determined by the complex interaction of molecular, environmental, and immunological variables. Every individual's path from genetic predisposition to environmental exposure and the ensuing immunological responses is different. Recognizing this diversity provides for a more nuanced perspective, underlining the importance of customized methods to controlling and minimizing the effects of salicylate sensitivity.

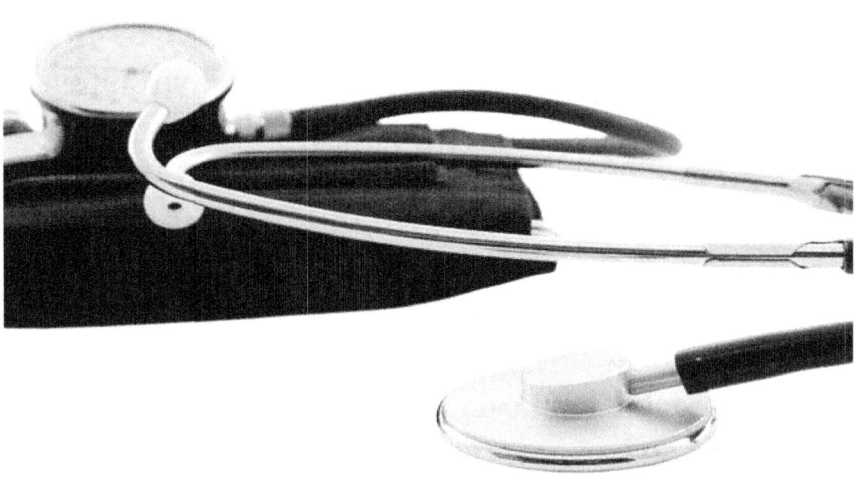

SYMPTOMS AND DIAGNOSIS

Salicylate sensitivity symptoms are broad and can affect a variety of organ systems. Common signs include gastrointestinal problems, skin sensitivities, and respiratory difficulties.

Making a diagnosis entails a thorough review of the patient's medical history, a thorough investigation of their symptoms, and perhaps provocative testing.

1. **CUTANEOUS MANIFESTATIONS: Skin as a Silent Communicator**

Salicylate sensitivity often reveals itself through a spectrum of cutaneous manifestations. Itchy skin, hives, or eczema like rashes are frequent signals that the body is reacting to heightened salicylate levels. Understanding the nuances of these skin reactions becomes crucial, as they often serve as the initial indicators of sensitivity.

2. **GASTROINTESTINAL DISTURBANCES: Managing issues with Digestion.**

Salicylate sensitivity can mostly affect the digestive system, resulting in symptoms including bloating, discomfort in the abdomen, and changes in bowel patterns. Despite their differences, these gastrointestinal disorders all have one thing in common: eating foods high in salicylates can frequently cause or aggravate them. Understanding the relationship between food decisions and digestive symptoms is essential to understanding the intricate web of salicylate sensitivity.

3. RESPIRATORY SYMPTOMS: Revealing the Quiet Agitator

Some people are more sensitive to salicylate, which might have an impact on their respiratory system. It is possible for symptoms to manifest as sinusitis, nasal congestion, or even asthma like symptoms.

Inhaling salicylate containing chemicals, which are commonly found in home goods or personal care products, might function as quiet agitators, compromising respiratory health.

4. SYSTEMIC REACTIONS: A Comprehensive Method for Handling Symptoms

Salicylate sensitivity is not limited to a few symptoms; it can show as a complex interaction of several body responses. More noticeable symptoms may be accompanied by fatigue, headaches, and a general sensation of malaise. This systemic approach to comprehending the larger impact of salicylate sensitivity emphasizes the need of identifying the linked nature of symptoms.

5. **DIAGNOSTIC JOURNEY: Identifying Symptoms and Seeking Explicit Information**

The path to a diagnosis entails a thorough examination of medical history, a complete symptom analysis, and, at times, provocative testing.

Understanding one's individual symptom profile is an important step in solving the puzzle of salicylate sensitivity. Individuals are guided through this diagnostic path by medical experts who are knowledgeable about possible triggers and have a thorough awareness of their symptoms.

6. **PROVOCATION TESTING: Elucidating Sensitivity via Difficulties**

Provocation testing is a diagnostic technique that entails a medically supervised, controlled exposure to drugs containing salicylate. This procedure enables healthcare practitioners to watch and assess the body's response, which aids in the confirmation of sensitivity. It is an essential part of the diagnostic process, giving those traversing the terrain of salicylate sensitivity direction and clarity.

Tips: To help readers traverse the diagnosis process, we provide them with the tools to identify possible symptoms, speak out for their health, and collaborate with medical specialists.

IMPACT ON DAILY LIFE

Managing Salicylate Sensitivity on a Day-to-Day Basis Beyond the constraints of medical settings, salicylate sensitivity has an impact on the complex fabric of daily living.

GROCERY SHOPPING

Grocery shopping is transformed, from a usual job to a strategic mission for people sensitive to salicylates. Navigating the aisles becomes a painstaking exercise of reading labels, deciphering ingredient lists, and detecting the presence of salicylates in ordinary goods. Individuals learn to become proficient label readers, discerning between permitted and trigger foods, creating a more empowered approach to their nutritional choices.

MEAL PREPARATION

Meal preparation becomes an exercise in culinary innovation while keeping salicylate sensitivity in mind. Individuals who must avoid specific components are more likely to experiment with alternative flavor enhancers, herbs, and spices that adhere to their dietary limitations. Exploring individuals' creative adjustments highlights that, despite the hurdles, a diversified and enjoyable diet is possible within the limits of salicylate sensitivity.

DIETARY DILEMMAS

Balancing dietary requirements with salicylate limitations becomes a difficult dance. Individuals with salicylate sensitivity frequently face the issue of maintaining a balanced diet while following to dietary restrictions. The emphasis is on nutritional concerns, offering insights into alternate food options that enable a well-rounded and nutritious approach to everyday nourishment.

SOCIAL AND EMOTIONAL IMPACT

Salicylate sensitivity has an influence on both physical and mental health.

Dining out, attending social gatherings, and sharing meals with friends and family can be difficult. Exploring social dynamics may help with effective communication, comprehension, and emotional resilience in the face of external impressions and misconceptions.

PRACTICAL STRATEGIES

Practical techniques are required to navigate the influence on one's everyday life. Individuals with salicylate sensitivity learn how to build resilience by following meal planning suggestions and communicating effectively with healthcare providers, as well as creating a supportive environment. Providing practical knowledge and empowers people in their daily lives, demonstrating that salicylate sensitivity can be overcome with educated decisions and adaptive methods.

IMPORTANCE OF DIETARY MANAGEMENT

Dietary management appears as a key component in the efficient treatment of salicylate sensitivity, extending beyond a simple list of banned items. A crucial part of the process is figuring out the nuances of mindful eating, where the science of sensitivity management and the art of feeding collide.

NAVIGATING MINDFUL FOOD CHOICES

Making thoughtful food selections becomes essential when dealing with salicylate sensitivity in the diet. Instead of concentrating only on limitations, people are encouraged to consider other, just as fulfilling possibilities. Exploring the skill of creating a varied and well-balanced meal while following salicylate restrictions highlights that the path is about accepting a rich tapestry of healthy options rather than just restriction.

ELIMINATION DIETS

Elimination diets, in which people set out on a concentrated quest to find and eliminate possible triggers, are essential to optimal nutritional control. Advice on creating individualized exclusion diets clarifies how to methodically cut out particular foods to determine how they affect sensitivity.

ELIMINATION DIETS are a tactical technique for managing salicylate sensitivity that is intended to locate and get rid of possible triggers. These diets, which are customized to meet the needs of each-individual, include gradually eliminating particular-items to determine how they affect sensitivity.

The following are popular elimination diets that people could think about:

- **Low Salicylate Diet**: This entails staying away from foods high in salicylates, such as certain vegetables (tomatoes, peppers), fruits (berries, grapes, oranges), and spices.

- **Feingold Diet:** This diet, which was first created for kids with attention issues, forbids artificial additives, salicylates, and certain food colorings.

- **FODMAP Elimination:** Although this approach is mostly intended for people with irritable bowel syndrome (IBS), some people who are sensitive to salicylates find relief by temporarily cutting out foods' rich in fructose, margarine, and polysaccharides, such as various fruits, vegetables, and grains.

- **Specific Carbohydrate Diet (SCD):** To treat diseases including Crohn's disease, this diet limits complex carbs. Because salicylate is restricting, some people who are sensitive to it find it helpful.

- **Paleolithic, also known as the Paleo diet:** This plan discourages the use of processed carbohydrates, grains, and legumes in favor of whole, unprocessed foods. It might be modified to omit foods rich in salicylate.

- **Rotation Diet:** Reduces the chance of acquiring sensitivities by rotating meals in a methodical manner. You can modify this diet to include low-salicylate foods.

- **Candida Diet:** This diet excludes processed foods, sweets, and gluten to lessen the overgrowth of Candida. Its limited approach may provide relief for certain persons who are sensitive to salicylates.

Note:

Before starting any elimination diet, it is recommended to speak with a medical practitioner or a certified dietitian. The efficacy of these diets can differ from person to person. Moreover, these diets are frequently followed by a phase of controlled reintroduction to evaluate tolerance and sensitivity on an individual basis, after which they are administered for a certain period of time.

GRADUAL REINTRODUCTION

The methodical procedure of progressively reintroducing meals after the elimination period is equally important. People can recover a rich and varied eating experience by learning the technique of reintroducing foods into their diets. A tailored route of gradual reintroduction reveals which foods may be welcomed without inciting sensitivity. It highlights that dietary decisions don't have to be fixed and may change over time to incorporate a variety of tastes and minerals.

GRADUAL REINTRODUCTION is an important step of salicylate sensitivity treatment after the elimination stage. It entails gradually reintroducing meals to find those that may be accepted without causing sensitivity. People may regain a rich and varied food experience with this customized trip.

Key components of a gradual reintroduction are as follows:

- **Reintroduce food things one by one:** This technology enables detailed observation of the body's reaction to each individual meal.

- **Keep a comprehensive food record during the reintroduction phase.** Take note of the items that were reintroduced, the quantity ingested, and any symptoms that occurred. This material helps to detect trends and triggers.

- **Gradual Increase in Complexity:** Start with meals that are low in salicylates and typically well tolerated. As tolerance develops, progressively introduce increasingly complex and potentially salicylate-rich meals.

- **Observe Symptoms:** Pay attention to physical and intestinal problems during reintroduction. This includes skin responses, gastrointestinal distress, respiratory problems, and any other indicators of sensitivity.

- **Interval Between Reintroduction:** Provide an adequate amount of time between reintroduction in order to precisely evaluate the body's reaction. This duration typically ranges from several days to a week, although it can differ from person to person.

- **Seeking Advice from Healthcare Professionals:** It is recommended to conduct the phase of progressive reintroduction with the supervision of a registered dietitian or healthcare professional. They can offer customized guidance and assistance according to specific health needs.

- **Adaptability and Flexibility:** Be aware that reactions to meals might differ and that the process of gradual reintroduction is unique. Be adaptable when modifying the reintroduction schedule in accordance with individual tolerance levels.

- **Integrate Variety:** Reintroduce a range of items to the diet gradually as tolerance is built. This measure guarantees that nutritional requirements are satisfied by encouraging a varied and well-balanced eating habit.

- **Honor Achievements:** Honor and celebrate effective reintroduction. People feel more powerful and driven when they increase the variety of foods they choose to eat because of this encouraging reinforcement.

- **Long-Term Lifestyle Changes:** Gradual reintroduction involves more than simply make-shift lifestyle changes. Stress the long term and urge people to think of food choices as flexible and changing, containing a range of nutrients and tastes.

T IPs:

The technique of gradual reintroduction is a customized and dynamic approach that seeks to achieve equilibrium between restoring dietary diversity and addressing sensitivity. When combined with expert advice, a methodical and deliberate approach can enable people to effectively traverse this stage of life.

SCAN QR TO PURCHASE A SYMPTOM TRACKER.

BEYOND SYMPTOM MANAGEMENT

When it comes to cultivating a lifestyle that is proactive and empowered, dietary control becomes an essential component. The investigation highlights the transforming potential of dietary strategies and encourages people to see them as proactive measures to improve overall wellness rather than only as a reaction to symptoms. With the means to not just control symptoms but also develop a way of living that honors nutrition and energy, people go through life with resiliency and vigor.

Here are key elements tools of this transformative journey:

- **Holistic sustenance:** Dietary techniques emphasize the body's holistic sustenance rather than just treating symptoms. People are urged to consider the role that their food choices have in supporting their general health by including a variety of nutrients.

- **Mindfulness in Eating Practices:** The investigation highlights how crucial mindful eating is. People can develop a closer relationship with their food and enjoy more satisfying meals when they eat mindfully and in the moment.

- **Psychological Empowerment:** Making dietary changes gives people the ability to actively manage their health. People feel more in charge and have more agency in controlling their salicylate sensitivity when they are aware of how their dietary decisions affect their health.

- **Responsive Lifestyle:** Dietary techniques urge people to modify their lifestyles to better suit their specific requirements. This flexible method affects daily activities, interpersonal relationships, and general lifestyle decisions in addition to the kitchen.

- **Building Resilience:** Dietary solutions could improve lives by fostering emotional and physical resilience. People gain the ability to overcome obstacles, recognize their accomplishments, and handle failure with poise.

- **Positive Reinforcement:** Dietary practices that are successfully implemented provide positive reinforcement. People celebrate accomplishments, such as reintroducing a favorite cuisine or continuing to eat a well-balanced diet that promotes vitality.

- **Long-Term Wellness:** The investigation highlights how dietary modifications have a long-term impact. People are taught to perceive dietary modifications as sustainable decisions that support continuous wellness rather than as short-term fixes.

- **Vibrancy Oriented Lifestyle:** Cultivating a lifestyle that honors vitality is the aim. Dietary methods become an important aspect of a vitality-focused lifestyle, encouraging energy, well-being, and a general sense of vibrancy.

ADVANCED GUIDANCE

People are recommended to seek expert advice from licensed nutritionists or medical practitioners along this trip. This assistance guarantees that food decisions are in line with personal health objectives and needs.

ENGAGING THE COMMUNITY

Community involvement has the potential to be revolutionary as well. People managing salicylate sensitivity are urged to make connections with people going through comparable difficulties, creating a network of support where people may exchange experiences, wisdom, and encouragement.

CHAPTER 2

UNVEILING SALICYLATE SOURCES

This chapter provides a thorough guide to navigating the different origins and presence of salicylates in various facets of our everyday life. Effective treatment requires an understanding of where salicylates lurk.

SALICYLATES FOUND IN MEDICAMENTS

Salicylates, widely known for their strong anti-inflammatory effects, are included in many pharmaceutical products. This section thoroughly investigates the long list of pharmaceuticals that include salicylates, which includes both prescription and easily accessible over-the-counter pain medicines. Those who are responsible for managing salicylate sensitivity must have a thorough awareness of the medical environment in order to make educated decisions about their treatment.

1. Anti Inflammatory Powerhouses

The capacity of salicylates, which are generated from salicylic acid, to lessen pain and inflammation has long been known. Although this renders them useful constituents in many pharmaceutical formulations, it also presents a difficulty for persons who are salicylate sensitive.

2. Painkillers available over the counter

Salicylates are widely included in over-the-counter pain medications, which people reach for during uncomfortable situations. Aspirin is a common example of a salicylate-containing drug that is well-known for its ability to reduce pain and inflammation. NSAIDs, or non-steroidal anti-inflammatory medicines, are another class of pharmaceuticals with a salicylate content that includes drugs like naproxen and ibuprofen.

3. Drugs on Prescription

Salicylates can also be found in prescription drugs that are used to treat particular medical disorders. Salicylates may be an ingredient in the formulation of several cardiovascular drugs, such as blood thinners. Moreover, salicylates may be found in rheumatoid arthritis drugs and dermatological therapies.

4. Charting the Medicinal Terrain

Managing salicylate sensitivity requires an understanding of the frequency of salicylates in drugs. It entails using a sophisticated approach to making judgments about medical treatment, considering both the possible influence on sensitivity and the intended therapeutic effects of a medicine. People are invited to:

NOTE:

• **Speak With Medical Professionals:** Those with salicylate sensitivity should speak with their medical specialists before starting any medicine. This lessens the possibility of causing sensitive reactions and guarantees that the drug of choice is in line with their medical requirements.

• **Carefully Read Labels:** It's important to read medicine labels with caution. Making educated decisions is made easier when people are aware of products that contain salicylate and their possible effects.

• **Consider Other Options:** Medical practitioners may consider other treatment options if salicylate-containing drugs are not appropriate. This might entail choosing drugs with a lower salicylate concentration or going with non-salicylate alternatives.

SALICYLATES IN FOODS

HIGH SALICYLATE FOODS

Embark on a complete adventure into the domain of high salicylate foods—a voyage that unravels the depth of tastes but also demands a discriminating attitude to dietary choices.

This section includes a comprehensive list of foods high in salicylates, including fruits, vegetables, spices, and herbs. As a preventative precaution against potential sensitivity triggers, identifying and comprehending these sources of high salicylate is essential to effective dietary control.

FRUITS:

Indulge in the rich variety of fruits, since their pleasing sweetness frequently masks the possibility of salicylic content. The complex world of high salicylate fruits is revealed in this investigation; each fruit has a distinct flavor profile and nutritional advantages, and some should be avoided by those who are sensitive.

- In addition to being nature's gems, **Berries** also include salicylate complexity. They are renowned for their vivid colors and antioxidant-rich profiles. Strawberries and blueberries are two fruit high in salicylate that entice with their sweet, tart flavor.

These little packets are full of nutrients, however for those who are sensitive, the salicylate level should be carefully considered.

- **CITRUS FRUITS:** Known for their acidic and cooling properties, citrus fruits bring a brilliant pop of color to the culinary palette. Tangerines and oranges, commonplace in many homes, exhibit subtleties in salicylate content. Their salicylic content encourages people to balance these pleasures with sensitivity considerations even if they provide vitamin C and a tart brightness.

- **STONE FRUITS**: Stone fruits are a summertime delight that should be consumed with caution due to salicylate concerns. Desserts and snacks gain a touch of refinement from the rich crimson attraction of cherries and the delicate sweetness of apricots. Though they have a rich appearance, people who are sensitive should exercise caution when handling these stone fruits due to their high salicylate content.

CONSIDERATIONS FOR NAVIGATING SENSITIVITY: CRAFTING A BALANCED PALETTE
These fruits with high salicylate content add to a complex tapestry of tastes, but because of their subtleties, those who are sensitive should proceed with caution:

DIVERSE FRUIT INTAKE: A well-balanced diet must include a range of fruits. Still, moderation takes precedence, enabling people to enjoy the fullness of tastes without overdoing the system with salicylate.

POSSIBILITIES: Low salicylate fruits, such peeled pears, mangos, bananas, and apples, offer a variety of possibilities for individuals looking to expand their fruit intake. These options strike a compromise between managing sensitivity and providing nutritional advantages.

INDIVIDUAL SENSITIVITY VARIATION: It is important to understand that sensitivity differs throughout individuals. Certain fruits with high salicylate content may cause symptoms in certain people, but others may be able to consume them in moderation. Creating a diet that prioritizes fruits while being mindful of sensitivity requires individualized observation and modification.

VEGETABLES:

Explore the world of veggies, a lush range of colorful greens and cruciferous marvels that mix to provide distinct flavors and nutritional advantages to the tongue. However, this green beauty conceals a layer of deep intricacy.

This disquisition unveils high salicylate vegetables, including tomatoes, peppers, and certain lush flora like spinach and kale. Understanding the nuanced choices in vegetables empowers individualities to draft reactions that celebrate flavor without compromising perceptivity operation.

- **TOMATOES:** Tomatoes are commonly used in cooking and have a rich flavor with salicylate undertones. Whether in sauces, salads, or sandwiches, their flexibility is unparalleled. However, for those with heightened sensitivity, the salicylate level of tomatoes necessitates a cautious approach to balancing culinary enjoyment with dietary concern.

- **PEPPERS:** A common ingredient in many culinary traditions, peppers are known for their vivid hues and range of intensity. However, the presence of salicylates complicates matters. From s to chili peppers, recognizing the salicylate differences in these colorful additions lets people adapt their spice preferences while avoiding sensitivity.

- **LEAFY GREENS**: While leafy greens are known for being high in nutrients, they also contain salicylates that should be considered. Spinach and kale, which are high in vitamins and minerals, enhance the elegance of salads and smoothies. However, because to its salicylic content, people who are sensitive should include them in moderation.

COOKING TECHNIQUES: Using different cooking methods, such as blanching or steaming, might help reduce salicylate concentrations in vegetables. These approaches maintain nutritional value while reducing possible sensitization triggers.

INDIVIDUALIZED ADAPTATION: Because individual sensitivity differs, a personalized approach to vegetable selection is required. Some people may find that some high salicylate vegetables are easily tolerated, whilst others may need to adapt their consumption based on specific reactions.

SPICES AND HERBS:

Spices and herbs enhance culinary experiences with distinct salicylate subtleties. The high salicylate content of herbs like mint and oregano, as well as spices like paprika, cumin, and cinnamon, is explained in this section. By recognizing these flavor enhancers, individuals can tailor their seasoning choices to align with their dietary restrictions.

- **CINNAMON:** Cinnamon is a versatile spice that adds warmth and comfort to a variety of meals, both sweet and savory. However, its salicylate-rich composition necessitates caution for individuals experiencing sensitivity.
- **CUMIN:** Cumin, known for its earthy and fragrant flavor, is commonly used in spice mixes. While it provides depth to foods, the presence of salicylate adds another level of complexity.
- **PAPRIKA:** Paprika, with its brilliant color and smokey overtones, is a versatile spice in various cuisines. However, the presence of salicylates necessitates caution. Exploring the salicylate-rich nature of paprika allows people to add a burst of color and flavor to their dishes while being sensitive to their culinary journey.
- **MINT:** Mint is a popular ingredient in both sweet and savory dishes due to its cooling properties. Despite its wonderful flavor, mint's salicylate

characteristics provide concerns for people who are sensitive.

- **OREGANO**: The leafy beauty of oregano makes it a classic in cooking that gives many foods their own unique flavor. However, its salicylate-rich nature necessitates a deliberate approach.

DIVERSE SPICE ALTERNATIVES: For those looking for alternatives, low-salicylate spices like fresh garlic, chives, and fennel provide a varied range of tastes. These options offer a rich tapestry of culinary expression while maintaining sensitivity control.

HOMEMADE BLENDS: Making homemade spice blends gives people control over the components. This enables the construction of tailored mixes that address both taste preferences and salicylate sensitivity.

VITAL STEPS IN DIETARY MANAGEMENT

The high salicylate foods are not just an experiment in taste; they are also a planned way to control your diet. To avoid possible allergy triggers, it's important to know what these high-salicylate foods are and stay away from them.

Important Key considerations include:

- **LABEL SCRUTINY:** It's very important to read labels carefully when shopping for both fresh food and boxed goods. Knowing what foods are high in salicylates helps people make smart food choices that meet their nutritional needs.

- **COOKING MODIFICATIONS:** If you are sensitive to salicylates, learning how to change the way you cook is very helpful. This may involve discovering alternative seasonings, picking low salicylate alternatives, or applying cooking methods that reduce salicylate concentrations.

- **BALANCING NUTRITIONAL NEEDS:** While avoiding high-salicylate foods is important, having a balanced diet is equally vital. This includes finding alternative, low salicylate choices to ensure nutritional needs are met without compromising sensitivity management.

LOW SALICYLATE FOODS

Explore the world of foods low in salicylate, which provides those who are sensitive with a plethora of alternatives that are less likely to cause symptoms. This section describes a variety of foods that form the basis of a low salicylate diet, providing important variety while reducing the risk of sensitivity triggers.

SALICYLATES IN HOUSEHOLD ITEMS

Salicylates, while prominent in foods, spread their reach beyond the plate, permeating various home items. From everyday cleaning products to personal care items, this part reveals the surprising sources of salicylates that lurk within our houses. Understanding these non-food sources is important for building a salicylate friendly environment and ensuring thorough sensitivity management.

- **CLEANING PRODUCTS:** Certain home cleaners, polishes, and disinfectants may contain salicylate-based chemicals. This part provides insights into deciphering labels and choosing alternative cleaning solutions to keep a salicylate conscious living space. Items like Laundry Detergent (arm + Hammer sensitive skin free & clear), EnviroRite products are also good.

Don't forget to Research about it and Ask questions? Because individuals react differently.

- **PERSONAL CARE ITEMS:** Delve into personal care items, where salicylates may unexpectedly find their way into products designed for skin and hair care. Lotions, shampoos, and even oral care products can harbor salicylate compounds. Dove Products (Bar soap can be recommended).

- **MEDICATED TOPICALS:** Even medicated topicals, designed for specific health issues, may contain salicylates. This includes creams, ointments, and patches made for pain relief or skin problems.

NON-FOOD SOURCES: Creating a Salicylate Friendly Environment
Crafting a salicylate friendly environment involves:

- **LABEL SCRUTINY:** Vigilantly reading labels on cleaning products and personal care items allows people to identify and avoid salicylate containing compounds. Choosing goods with clear labeling becomes a key aspect of having a salicylate friendly home.

ALTERNATIVE CHOICES: Seeking salicylate free alternatives for cleaning and personal care allows people to keep a healthy living area without losing sensitivity management. Many natural and safe choices are available for consideration.

CONSULTATION WITH HEALTHCARE PROFESSIONALS:

For individuals with heightened sensitivity, speaking with healthcare professionals or specialists can provide personalized suggestions for suitable home and personal care items.

This ensures that choices match with both health and sensitive needs.

WITHDRAWAL SYMPTOMS

Withdrawal symptoms are common when you initially start any of the diets and are typically an indication that the diet is working.

These might manifest as **headaches, dizziness, nausea, an infection, hangover-like sensations,** or just a worsening of the symptoms you are attempting to manage. Four or five days is all that these symptoms might linger before they normally go away and a noticeable improvement in health is seen.

You might have to wait longer, though, if the sickness is chronic, **Seek for medical attention from a professional**.

Psychologically, you can experience **anxiety** and **depression, lack enthusiasm**, and have a **short temper**. Recognize that this is normal and that your body is simply giving you one final glimpse at what has been stifled, buried, and ignored in the past and is now opening.

Recognize that these emotions are fleeting as well.

Accept them without judgment; **be "still"** and give **yourself permission to feel them**. Then, you'll be astounded at how rapidly they vanish.

WALKING, DEEP BREATHING, AND DRINKING A GLASS OF WATER CAN ALL BE BENEFICIAL.

SCAN QR TO VIEW LIST CONTAINING SALICYLATE SENSITIVITY.

CHAPTER 3

BREAKFAST & SMOOTHIE

Banana Oat Pancakes

Prep Time: 15 minutes

Servings: 4

Ingredients:

1 cup rice flour or wheat flour

1/2 cup oat flour

1 ripe banana, mashed

1 cup milk (or a non-dairy alternative)

1 tablespoon white sugar

1 teaspoon baking powder

Pinch of salt

canola oil for cooking

Instructions:

In a mixing bowl, combine rice flour, oat flour, mashed banana, milk, sugar, baking powder, and a pinch of salt until a smooth batter forms.

Heat coconut oil in a pan over medium heat.

Spoon pancake batter onto the pan and cook until bubbles appear on the surface. Flip and cook until golden brown.

Serve with sliced pear (peeled) and a drizzle of maple syrup.

Rice Flour Waffles with Maple Syrup

Prep Time: 20 minutes

Servings: 4

Ingredients:

2 cups rice flour

1 tablespoon baking powder

1 1/2 cups rice milk

2 tablespoons melted coconut oil

2 tablespoons white sugar

1 teaspoon Malta extract

Instructions:

Set your waffle iron according to the manufacturer's instructions.

In a large bowl, whisk together rice flour, baking powder, rice milk, melted coconut oil, sugar, and Malta extract until smooth.

Pour the batter onto the preheated waffle iron and cook until golden brown and crisp.

Serve warm with a drizzle of maple syrup.

Papaya Breakfast Bowl

Prep Time: 15 minutes
Servings: 2
Ingredients:
1 cup diced papaya
1/2 cup rice flakes
2 tablespoons white sugar
1 cup rice milk
Instructions:
In a bowl, mix diced papaya, rice flakes, and white sugar.
Pour rice milk over the mixture.
Stir well and let it sit for a few minutes before enjoying.

Pecan and Banana Bread

Prep Time: 15 minutes (+ baking time)
Servings: 8
Ingredients:
1 1/2 cups rice flour
1/2 cup chopped pecans
2 ripe bananas, mashed
1/2 cup white sugar
1/2 cup melted canola oil
2 eggs
1 teaspoon malta extract (optional)

Instructions:
Set the oven temperature to 350°F (175°C). Grease a loaf pan.

In a bowl, combine rice flour, chopped pecans, mashed bananas, sugar, melted coconut oil, eggs, and Malta extract.

Mix until well combined and pour into the prepared loaf pan.

Bake for 50 60 minutes or until a toothpick inserted into the center comes out clean.

Allow to cool before slicing.

Mango Smoothie Bowl
Prep Time: 10 minutes
Servings: 1
Ingredients:
1 cup diced mango
1/2 banana, sliced
2 tablespoons coconut flakes
1/2 cup coconut milk
Granola for topping (low salicylate)
Instructions:
In a blender, combine diced mango, banana slices, coconut flakes, and coconut milk.

Blend until smooth.

Pour the smoothie into a bowl.

Top with additional diced mango, banana slices, and granola.

Enjoy with a spoon for a refreshing and satisfying breakfast.

Tofu Scramble with Vegetables

Prep Time: 10 minutes
Cook Time: 10 minutes
Servings: 2
Ingredients:
1 tablespoon Canola oil
1/2 leek, diced (optional)
1/2 carrot, peeled and diced
1 block firm tofu, crumbled
1 teaspoon Garlic powder
Salt to taste
Fresh herbs (parsley, chives) for garnish
Instructions:
In a pan, sauté leek, and carrot in canola oil until softened.

Add crumbled tofu, garlic, and salt. Cook until heated through.

Garnish with fresh herbs before serving.

Whole Grain Pancakes with Fruit Compote

Prep Time: 15 minutes

Cook Time: 15 minutes

Servings: 4

Ingredients:

1 cup whole wheat flour

1 tablespoon baking powder

1 tablespoon maple syrup

1 cup coconut milk (unsweetened)

1 teaspoon Malta extract

Mixed fruit compote (banana, peeled pears) for topping

Instructions:

In a bowl, mix whole wheat flour and baking powder.

Add maple syrup, coconut milk, and Malta extract. Stir until well combined.

Pour batter onto a hot griddle and cook until bubbles form on the surface. Flip and cook until golden.

Serve with mixed fruit compote.

Lavender Stress Relief Tea

Prep Time: 5 minutes

Servings: 1

Ingredients:

1 teaspoon dried lavender buds

1 cup hot water

Chamomile honey (optional)

Instructions:

Steep dried lavender buds in hot water for 5-7 minutes.

Strain the herbs and add chamomile honey if desired.

Chocolate Banana Protein Smoothie

Prep Time: 5 minutes

Servings: 2

Ingredients:

2 bananas, frozen

2 tablespoons cocoa powder

1 cup milk (unsweetened)

1 scoop plant based protein powder

1 tablespoon cashew butter

Ice cubes (optional)

Instructions:

Blend frozen bananas, cocoa powder, milk, plant based protein powder, and cashew butter until smooth.

Add ice cubes if desired.

Banana Pancakes

Prep Time: 10 minutes

Cook Time: 10 minutes

Servings: 2

Ingredients:

2 ripe bananas, mashed

2 eggs

1/2 cup rice flour

1 teaspoon baking powder

1/2 teaspoon banana extract

Maple syrup for topping

Instructions:

In a bowl, combine mashed bananas, eggs, rice flour, baking powder, and banana extract.

Heat a griddle and spoon batter onto it to form pancakes. Cook until bubbles form on the surface, then flip and cook until golden.

Serve with a drizzle of maple syrup.

Soy Flour Banana Bread

Prep Time: 15 minutes
Cook Time: 50 minutes
Servings: 8
Ingredients:
2 cups Soy Flour
1 teaspoon Baking Powder
1/2 teaspoon Baking Soda
1/2 teaspoon Salt
3 large Bananas, mashed
1/2 cup canola Oil
1 cup White Sugar
2 large Eggs
1 teaspoon banana Extract
Instructions:
Set the oven temperature to 350°F (175°C) and grease a loaf pan.

In a bowl, whisk together soy flour, baking powder, baking soda, and salt.

In another bowl, combine mashed bananas, canola oil, sugar, eggs, and banana extract.

Add the wet ingredients to the dry ingredients and mix until well combined.

Pour the batter into the prepared loaf pan and bake for 45 50 minutes or until a toothpick inserted comes out clean.

Rice Flour and Cashew Porridge

Prep Time: 10 minutes
Cook Time: 15 minutes
Servings: 2
Ingredients:
1 cup Rice Flour
2 cups Milk
1/4 cup Cashews, chopped
1 tablespoon White Sugar (optional)
Instructions:
In a saucepan, combine rice flour and milk.
Cook over medium heat, stirring continuously until the mixture thickens.
Stir in chopped cashews and sugar if desired.
Serve hot.

Hazelnut and Pear French Toast

Prep Time: 15 minutes
Cook Time: 10 minutes
Servings: 4
Ingredients:
8 slices Rye Flour Bread
2 large Eggs
1/2 cup Hazelnuts, finely ground
1 cup Milk

1 teaspoon banana Extract

1 Canned Pear (in light syrup), sliced

Maple Syrup (moderate salicylate sweetener, for drizzling)

Instructions:

In a shallow bowl, whisk together eggs, ground hazelnuts, milk, and banana extract.

Dip each slice of rye flour bread into the mixture, ensuring both sides are coated.

Cook on a griddle or nonstick pan over medium heat until golden brown on both sides.

Top with sliced canned pear and drizzle with maple syrup.

Poppy Seed and Banana Muffins

Prep Time: 15 minutes

Cook Time: 20 minutes

Servings: 6

Ingredients:

1 cup Rice Flour

1/4 cup Poppy Seeds

1/2 cup Sugar (granulated)

2 teaspoons Baking Powder

1/2 teaspoon Salt

2 large Bananas, mashed

1/2 cup Milk

1/4 cup sunflower Oil

Instructions:

Set the oven temperature to 375°F (190°C) and line a muffin tin with paper liners.

In a large bowl, combine rice flour, poppy seeds, sugar, baking powder, and salt.

In another bowl, mix mashed bananas, milk, and sunflower oil.

Combine wet and dry ingredients.

Spoon the batter into muffin cups and bake for 18 20 minutes.

CHAPTER 4

LUNCH RECIPES

Rice and Lentil Salad Bowl
Prep Time: 15 minutes
Servings: 2
Ingredients:
1 cup Cooked Brown Rice
1/2 cup Cooked Green Lentils
1/4 cup Chopped Chives
1/4 cup Bamboo Shoots (sliced)
2 tablespoons Malt Vinegar
Salt to taste
Instructions:
In a large glass bowl, combine cooked brown rice, green lentils, chives, and bamboo shoots.
Drizzle malt vinegar over the salad and toss gently.
Season with salt according to taste.
Serve immediately or refrigerate for later.

Potato and Leek Soup

Prep Time: 30 minutes
Servings: 4
Ingredients:
3 cups Peeled and Diced Potatoes
1 cup Chopped Leeks
4 cups Water or Low Salicylate Vegetable Broth
1/4 cup Tapioca
Salt to taste
Instructions:
In a large pot, combine potatoes, leeks, water or vegetable broth, and tapioca.
Bring to a boil, then reduce heat and simmer until potatoes are tender.
Use a blender to puree the soup until smooth.
Season with salt to taste.
Serve hot.

Malt Glazed Salmon

Prep Time: 25 minutes
Servings: 2
Ingredients:
2 Salmon Fillets
2 tablespoons Malt Extract

1 tablespoon Soy Sauce (not low sodium)

1 tablespoon Rice Vinegar

Salt to taste

Instructions:

Set the oven temperature to 400°F (200°C).

In a bowl, mix malt extract, soy sauce, and rice vinegar.

Place salmon fillets on a baking sheet and brush the glaze over them.

Season with salt and pepper.

Bake for 15-18 minutes or until the salmon is cooked through.

Serve hot.

Lentil and Potato Patties

Prep Time: 30 minutes

Servings: 4

Ingredients:

1 cup Cooked Yellow Split Peas

1 cup Mashed Potatoes

1/4 cup Chopped Chives

1/4 cup Tapioca

Sunflower Oil (for frying)

Instructions:
In a large bowl, combine cooked yellow split peas, mashed potatoes, chives, and tapioca.
Shape the mixture into patties.
Heat sunflower oil in a pan over medium heat.
Fry the patties until golden brown on both sides.
Serve with a side of green salad.

Borlotti Bean and Rice Bowl
Prep Time: 25 minutes
Servings: 2
Ingredients:
1 cup Cooked Borlotti Beans
1 cup Cooked White Rice
1/2 cup Sliced Bamboo Shoots
2 tablespoons Malt Vinegar
Salt to taste
Instructions:
In a bowl, combine cooked borlotti beans, white rice, bamboo shoots, malt vinegar, and salt.
Toss gently until well mixed.
Serve warm or at room temperature.

Hazelnut Crusted Chicken Tenders

Prep Time: 25 minutes

Servings: 3

Ingredients:

1 lb Chicken Tenders

1/2 cup Hazelnuts (finely chopped)

2 tablespoons Tapioca

Salt to taste

Sunflower Oil (for frying)

Instructions:

In a bowl, mix chopped hazelnuts, tapioca, salt, and pepper.

Coat each chicken tender in the hazelnut mixture.

Heat sunflower oil in a skillet over medium heat.

Fry the chicken tenders until golden brown on all sides.

Serve with a side of green beans.

Mango and Chicken Lettuce Wraps

Prep Time: 20 minutes

Servings: 2

Ingredients:

1 cup Cooked and Shredded Chicken Breast

1 Mango (peeled and diced)

1 cup Iceberg Lettuce Leaves

2 tablespoons Malt Vinegar

Salt to taste
Instructions:
Combine shredded chicken, diced mango, and malt vinegar in a large bowl for easy mixture.
Season with salt to taste.
Spoon the mixture onto individual iceberg lettuce leaves.
Serve as wraps.

Pear and Walnut Salad
Prep Time: 15 minutes
Servings: 2
Ingredients:
2 Pears (peeled and sliced)
1/2 cup Walnuts (chopped)
1 cup Iceberg Lettuce (torn into bite sized pieces)
2 tablespoons White Sugar
1 tablespoon Malt Vinegar
Instructions:
In a large salad bowl, combine sliced pears, chopped walnuts, and torn iceberg lettuce.
Sprinkle little white sugar over the salad.
Drizzle malt vinegar over the mixture and toss gently.
Serve immediately.

Chive and Potato Hash Browns

Prep Time: 20 minutes

Servings: 4

Ingredients:

2 cups Grated Old White Potatoes

1/4 cup Chopped Chives

1/4 cup Tapioca

Sunflower Oil (for frying)

Salt to taste

Instructions:

Wrap the shredded potatoes on a clean kitchen towel.

Lightly squeeze out the potatoes to remove excess water from it.

In a bowl, combine grated potatoes, chives, and tapioca.

Heat sunflower oil in a skillet over medium heat.

Spoon the potato mixture into the skillet to form hash browns.

Cook until golden brown on both sides.

Season with Salt to taste.

Serve hot.

Pumpkin Seed and Chickpea Hummus
Prep Time: 15 minutes
Servings: 6
Ingredients:
1 can Chickpeas (drained and rinsed)
1/4 cup Pumpkin Seeds
2 tablespoons Malt Vinegar
1 clove Garlic (minced)
Salt to taste
Sunflower Oil (for drizzling)
Instructions:
In a food processor, blend chickpeas, pumpkin seeds, malt vinegar, minced garlic, and salt until smooth.
Drizzle sunflower oil over the hummus.
Serve with vegetable sticks or gluten free crackers.

Tamarillo and Papaya Salsa
Prep Time: 15 minutes
Servings: 4
Ingredients:
1 Tamarillo (peeled and diced)
1/2 cup Diced Papaya
2 tablespoons Chopped Fresh Coriander

1 tablespoon Lime Juice
Salt to taste
Instructions:
In a bowl, combine diced tamarillo, diced papaya, chopped fresh coriander, lime juice, and salt.
Toss gently until well mixed.
Serve as a refreshing salsa.

DINNER RECIPES

Mango Glazed Chicken Skewers
Prep Time: 25 minutes
Servings: 3
Ingredients:
1 lb Chicken Breast (cut into cubes)
1 Mango (peeled and pureed)
2 tablespoons Malt Vinegar
1 tablespoon Soy Sauce (not low sodium)
1/4 cup Tapioca
Skewers for grilling
Instructions:
In a bowl, combine chicken cubes, mango puree, malt vinegar, soy sauce, and tapioca.
Thread the marinated chicken onto skewers.
Grill the skewers until the chicken is cooked through.
Baste with extra mango glaze while grilling.
Serve hot.

Pear and Walnut Stuffed Chicken Breast

Prep Time: 35 minutes

Servings: 2

Ingredients:

2 Chicken Breasts (boneless, skinless)

1 Pear (peeled and diced)

1/4 cup Chopped Walnuts

2 tablespoons Malt Vinegar

1/4 cup Tapioca

Salt to taste

Instructions:

Set the oven temperature to 375°F (190°C).

In a large bowl, mix diced pear, chopped walnuts, malt vinegar, tapioca, salt, and pepper.

Cut a pocket in each chicken breast and stuff with the pear and walnut mixture.

Secure the pockets with toothpicks.

Bake for 25 30 minutes or until the chicken is cooked through.

Remove toothpicks before serving.

Borlotti Bean and Chive Risotto

Prep Time: 35 minutes

Servings: 4

Ingredients:

1 cup Arborio Rice

1/2 cup Cooked Borlotti Beans

1/4 cup Chopped Chives

1/4 cup Tapioca

4 cups Low Salicylate Vegetable Broth

Salt to taste

Instructions:

In a pot, heat vegetable broth over medium heat.

In a separate pan, sauté Arborio rice with tapioca until translucent.

Gradually add the warm broth, stirring continuously until the rice is cooked.

Stir in borlotti beans, chives, salt, and pepper.

Continue cooking until the risotto reaches a creamy consistency.

Serve hot.

Tapioca Crusted Tofu Stir Fry

Prep Time: 25 minutes

Servings: 3

Ingredients:

1 block Extra Firm Tofu (pressed and cubed)

1/4 cup Tapioca

2 tablespoons Soy Sauce (not low sodium)

1 tablespoon Sunflower Oil

1 cup String Beans (trimmed)

1/2 cup Sliced Bamboo Shoots

Salt to taste

Instructions:

Toss tofu cubes in tapioca until coated.

Heat sunflower oil in a wok or skillet over medium high heat.

Stir fry tofu until golden brown.

Add string beans and bamboo shoots to the pan and continue stir frying.

Pour soy sauce over the mixture and season with salt and pepper.

Serve hot over rice.

Apple Butter Glazed Chicken Thighs

Prep Time: 30 minutes

Servings: 4

Ingredients:

4 Chicken Thighs (bone in, skin on)

2 tablespoons Homemade Apple Butter

1 tablespoon Malt Vinegar

1/4 cup Tapioca

Salt to taste

Instructions:

Set the oven temperature to 400°F (200°C).

In a bowl, mix apple butter, malt vinegar, tapioca, salt, and pepper.

Coat chicken thighs with the mixture.

Place the chicken in a baking dish and bake for 25 30 minutes or until cooked through.

Serve hot.

Lemon Garlic Shrimp and Sago Pilaf

Prep Time: 25 minutes

Servings: 2

Ingredients:

1 cup Sago

1/2 lb Shrimp (peeled and deveined)

1 Lemon (zested and juiced)
2 cloves Garlic (minced)
2 tablespoons Sunflower Oil
Salt to taste
Instructions:
Cook sago according to package instructions.
In a skillet, heat sunflower oil over medium heat.
Add shrimp, minced garlic, lemon zest, and lemon juice.
Cook until the shrimp is pink and opaque.
Fluff cooked sago with a fork and served with the lemon garlic shrimp on top.

Rye Flour and Leek Savory Pancakes
Prep Time: 20 minutes
Servings: 4
Ingredients:
1 cup Rye Flour
1 Leek (cleaned and thinly sliced)
1/4 cup Tapioca
1/2 cup Water
Sunflower Oil (for frying)
Instructions:
In a mixing bowl, combine rye flour, sliced leeks, tapioca, and water to form a batter.
Heat sunflower oil in a skillet over medium heat.

Spoon the batter onto the skillet to form pancakes.
Cook until golden brown on both sides.
Serve warm as a side dish or main course.

Rye Flour Pizza with Tomato Free Sauce
Prep Time: 40 minutes
Servings: 2
Ingredients:
Pizza Dough made with Rye Flour
1/2 cup Tomato Free Sauce (made with permissible ingredients)
1/2 cup Sliced Choko
1/4 cup Sliced Black Olives
1/4 cup Chopped Chives
Salt to taste
Instructions:
Set the oven temperature according to the pizza dough instructions.
Roll out the pizza dough on a floured surface.
Spread the tomato free sauce over the dough.
Top with sliced choko, black olives, and chopped chives.
Bake according to the pizza dough instructions.
Season with salt to taste.

Poppy Seed Crusted Fish Fillets

Prep Time: 20 minutes

Servings: 2

Ingredients:

2 White Fish Fillets

2 tablespoons Poppy Seeds

1/4 cup Rice Flour

2 tablespoons Sunflower Oil

Salt and Lemon Wedges for serving

Instructions:

Pat the fish fillets dry with a paper towel.

Mix poppy seeds and rice flour on a plate.

Press the fish fillets into the mixture, coating both sides.

Heat sunflower oil in a skillet over medium heat.

Cook the fish fillets for 3 4 minutes per side or until golden brown and cooked through.

Season with salt and serve with lemon wedges.

SNACKS & SYRUP

Maple Flavored Simple Syrup
Ingredients:
1/2 cup White Sugar
1/2 cup Water
1/2 teaspoon Maple Extract
Instructions:
In a saucepan, combine white sugar and water.
Heat over medium heat, stirring until the sugar dissolves.
Simmer for 5 minutes, then remove from heat.
Stir in the maple extract and let it cool before using.
Store in a sealed container in the refrigerator for up to one month.

Homemade Apple Chips
Prep Time: 3 hours
Servings: 4
Ingredients:
2 Apples (peeled and thinly sliced)
1 tablespoon White Sugar
Instructions:

Set the oven temperature to 200°F (93°C).
Place the apple slices on a baking sheet lined with parchment paper.
Sprinkle white sugar over the apple slices.
Bake for 2 3 hours or until the chips are crispy.
Allow to cool before serving.

Cashew and Sunflower Seed Energy Bites
Prep Time: 15 minutes
Servings: 12 bites
Ingredients:
1/2 cup Cashews (finely chopped)
1/4 cup Sunflower Seeds
2 tablespoons Maple Syrup
1/4 cup Tapioca
1/2 teaspoon Vanilla Extract
Desiccated Coconut (for rolling, optional)
Instructions:
In a food processor, combine chopped cashews, sunflower seeds, maple syrup, tapioca, and vanilla extract.
Pulse until the mixture forms a sticky dough.
Roll the mixture into small balls.
Optional: Roll the balls in desiccated coconut.
Refrigerate for at least 30 minutes before serving.

Carob Dipped Banana Chips

Prep Time: 15 minutes
Freezing Time: 1 2 hours
Servings: About 20 banana chips
Ingredients:

2 Bananas (peeled and sliced)

1/4 cup Carob Powder

2 tablespoons Maple Syrup

1/4 cup Desiccated Coconut (optional)

Instructions:

In a small bowl, mix carob powder and maple syrup to create a smooth dip.

Dip each banana slice into the carob mixture.

Optional: Roll the dipped banana slices in desiccated coconut.

Place on a parchment lined tray and freeze for 1 2 hours before serving.

Malt Syrup

Ingredients:

1 cup Malt Extract

1/4 cup Water

Instructions:

In a small saucepan, combine malt extract and water.

Heat over low heat, stirring constantly, until the malt extract is fully dissolved.

Allow the syrup to cool before using.

Store in a sealed container in the refrigerator for up to two weeks.

Hazelnut and Pecan Trail Mix
Prep Time: 10 minutes
Servings: About 2 cups
Ingredients:
1/2 cup Hazelnuts
1/2 cup Pecans
1/4 cup Dried Apricots (chopped)
1/4 cup Pumpkin Seeds
1/4 cup Sunflower Seeds
Instructions:
In a dry skillet, toast hazelnuts, pecans, pumpkin seeds, and sunflower seeds until fragrant.

Allow the nuts and seeds to cool completely.

Mix in the chopped dried apricots.

Store in an airtight container for a quick and nutritious snack.

Rice Cake with Soy Butter and Sliced Pear

Prep Time: 5 minutes
Servings: 4 servings

Ingredients:

Rice Cakes
Soy Butter
1 Pear (peeled and sliced)
1 tablespoon Maple Syrup (optional)

Instructions:

Spread soy butter over rice cakes.
Top each rice cake with slices of pear.
Drizzle with maple syrup if desired.
Serve as a quick and satisfying snack.

Hummus

Ingredients:

125g canned chickpeas, rinsed and drained
1/4 cup raw cashew nuts
1/4 cup pureed pears in syrup
2 garlic cloves, crushed
2 tablespoons canola oil

½ tsp salt

Instructions:

Combine all ingredients in a food processor and process until smooth.

Cashew Nut Butter

Prep Time: 3-5 minutes

Servings:

Ingredients

1/2 cup roasted cashew nuts

1/2 cup roasted chickpeas

1 2 tsp sunflower or canola oil

½ tsp salt (optional)

Instructions:

Combine all ingredients in a food processor and process until smooth.

Dear Friend,

I hope this letter finds you in good health and high spirits. I wanted to take a moment to express my heartfelt gratitude for your purchase of the Salicylate Sensitivity cookbook. Your support not only encourages me as an author but also contributes to spreading the message of healthy living and nourishing our bodies through mindful eating.

Thank you for choosing the Salicylate Sensitivity cookbook as your guide to a healthier lifestyle. By investing in this book, you have taken a proactive step towards improving your well-being and embracing a diet that promotes vitality and heart health. I am truly honored to be a part of your journey.

Within the pages of this cookbook, you will discover a treasure trove of delicious and nutritious recipes carefully crafted to support your health goals. Each recipe is designed to tantalize your taste buds while adhering to the principles of the Salicylate Sensitivity, providing you with a wide array of options to explore and savor.

I want to assure you that every recipe has been meticulously tested and developed with utmost care. My aim was to create a collection that not only offers a variety of flavors but also makes it easy for you to incorporate the Salicylate Sensitivity into your daily routine. It is my hope that these recipes will inspire you to experiment, enjoy the process of cooking, and discover the immense pleasure of nourishing yourself and your loved ones.

As you embark on this culinary adventure, I encourage you to remember the importance of balance and self care. The Salicylate Sensitivity is not just about the food we eat but also about adopting a holistic approach to our wellbeing. Prioritize regular exercise, stress management, and foster meaningful connections with those around you. By integrating these practices into your life, you can experience the full benefits of this transformative lifestyle.

In these challenging times, I would like to extend my warmest wishes for your continued health and safety. Please take care of yourself and your loved ones, and remember to embrace joy, gratitude, and the simple pleasures that life offers.

Once again, thank you for choosing the Salicylate Sensitivity cookbook. Your support means the world to me, and I hope this book becomes a trusted companion on your journey towards a healthier and more fulfilling life.

Stay safe and healthy, and may your culinary endeavors be filled with delight and nourishment.

With sincere appreciation,
Curnow K. Rivers

CONCLUSION

In conclusion, the "Salicylate Sensitivity Cookbook' extends far beyond a collection of recipes; it's a road map to rediscovering the joy of eating for those navigating salicylate sensitivity.

Through these pages, we've explored diverse ingredients, innovative cooking methods, and mouthwatering dishes, all centered on the belief that dietary restrictions should never compromise flavor.

This cookbook is not just a guide; it's a celebration of resilience and creativity, offering a wide array of options to make every meal enjoyable without triggering sensitivities. From breakfast to dinner, each recipe reflects a commitment to crafting satisfying meals within the boundaries of low salicylate living.

Beyond the kitchen, this book is an invitation to foster a deeper connection with one's body and respond to its unique needs with thoughtful nourishment.

It stands as a companion for those seeking a balance between health and indulgence, providing inspiration and variety for a well-rounded, satisfying diet.

As we close this culinary exploration, may the "Salicylate Sensitivity Cookbook" continue to be a source of inspiration, empowering individuals to savor each bite and embrace the shared joy of wholesome cooking. Here's to a life well-nourished and a kitchen filled with delicious possibilities.

7-DAY MEAL PLAN

Day 1:
Breakfast: Quinoa Porridge
Lunch: Lentil and Chive Salad
Dinner: Baked Salmon with Hazelnut Crust

Day 2:
Breakfast: Buckwheat Pancakes
Lunch: Turkey Wraps
Dinner: Borlotti Bean and Chive Risotto

Day 3:
Breakfast: Mango and Passion Fruit Smoothie
Lunch: Rice Noodle Salad
Dinner: Apple Butter Glazed Chicken Thighs

Day 4:
Breakfast: Oatmeal
Lunch: Tofu and Choko Stir Fry
Dinner: Quinoa Stuffed s

Day 5:
Breakfast: Poppy Seed Muffins
Lunch: Potato and Lentil Soup
Dinner: Baked Chicken Breast

Day 6:
Breakfast: Cashew Butter Smoothie
Lunch: Malt Vinegar Glazed Cod Fish Tacos
Dinner: Stir Fried Shrimp and Chives
Day 7:
Breakfast: Rice Flour Pancakes
Lunch: Chickpea Salad
Dinner: Beef and Potato Stew

Happy cooking and happy eating!

BONUS

Simple Exercises

Starting a fitness adventure while controlling salicylate sensitivity necessitates careful planning and specialized methods. We'll go over easy-to-do workouts that will help you remain in shape and be active without making you more sensitive.

Selecting The Appropriate Workouts

There are differences in workouts based on salicylate sensitivity. Choose cardiovascular health-promoting, low-impact activities that don't put you under unnecessary stress. Cycling, swimming, and walking are all great options. Investigate holistic approaches to exercise by participating in yoga or tai chi, which place an emphasis on balance and flexibility. (YouTube videos are a terrific resource to assist in setting up a beginner-friendly business).

Recognizing Your Body's Indications

It's crucial to pay attention to your body. Keep a watchful eye out for any indications of pain during or after activity. If you encounter negative effects, reevaluate the level of difficulty or any kind of exercise.

Introduce new workouts gradually while keeping an eye on your body's reaction. By taking a conscious approach, you may minimize possible triggers and yet reap the advantages of physical activity.

Easy Workouts for Daily Well-Being

1. **Stretching in the Morning:** Begin your day with a few lights stretches. Concentrate on each main muscle group, allowing 15–30 seconds to pass between each stretch. This establishes a pleasant attitude for the day and aids flexibility improvement.

2. **Yoga for Relaxation:** Try out some beginner-friendly yoga positions that put an emphasis on soft movements and relaxation. Yoga and other practices like restorative yoga or yin yoga can help you both mentally and physically without overstressing your body.

3. **Walking Meditation:** Incorporate mindfulness with the health advantages of walking. Enjoy a leisurely stroll while being mindful of your surroundings and each step you take. This kind of meditation can improve mental and physical health.

4. **Water Aerobics:** For a low-impact cardiovascular exercise, think about water aerobics. Water's buoyancy provides resistance for the activation of muscles while lessening the strain on joints. Those who are sensitive would especially benefit from this.

Advice for People Sensitive to Salicylates When Eating Out

The following useful advice can help guarantee a pleasurable eating experience:

1. **Do advanced research on restaurants:** Before going out to eat, look out for places that can accommodate special dietary needs. Menu samples and online reviews might give you an idea of what they have to offer.

2. **Clearly Communicate Dietary Needs:** Inform the server of your dietary requirements while placing your order. Please list any ingredients you must not eat, and feel free to enquire about the cooking techniques.

3. **Emphasize basic, Fresh Ingredients:** Choose recipes that highlight basic, fresh ingredients. Steamed or grilled foods with little flavor are frequently safer selections.

4. **Watch Out for Sauces and Marinades:** These substances may include unseen amounts of salicylates.
To limit how much you eat, request dishes without these extras or ask for them separately.
5. **Select Low Salicylate Options:** Pay attention to menu options that are inherently lower in salicylate. Lean meats, unadorned veggies, and carbohydrates like rice or potatoes may be examples of this.
6. **BYO Salad Dressing:** You might want **to bring a little jar** of your own low-salicylate salad dressing. This guarantees you a tasty and safe salad alternative.
7. **Speak Up for Your Needs:** Don't be afraid to speak up for what you need. If a restaurant is informed in advance of any dietary requirements, many of them will make accommodations.
8. **Show Gratitude:** Tell the **staff how much you appreciate them when they meet your demands at a restaurant**. This encouraging reaction motivates businesses to keep providing inclusive eating options.

FOR ADVICE AND QUESTIONS, SEND AN EMAIL TO:

Thank you,

And

Remember to Stay Safe and Healthy Always.

Printed in Great Britain
by Amazon